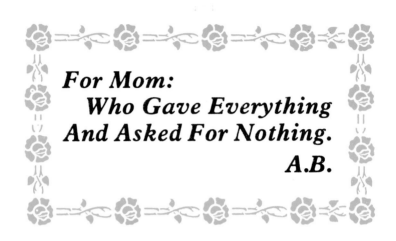

For Mom:
Who Gave Everything
And Asked For Nothing.
A.B.

Photography

Dr. Herbert R. Axelrod: 13, 32, 51; H. Hansen, Aquarium Berlin: 35; Richard Law: 15; Midori Shobo, Fish Magazine, Japan: 5; 7; 9; 11; 21; 27; 29; 31; 34; 39; 43; 46; 47; 50; Aaron Norman: 38; H.J. Richter: 42; A. Roth - Endpapers: 20; 25; Yoshida Fish Farms: 26.

A Beginner's Guide to
Goldfish

Written By
Anmarie Barrie

Contents

© 1986 by T.F.H. Publications, Inc. Distributed in the UNITED STATES by T.F.H. Publications, Inc., 211 West Sylvania Avenue, Neptune City, NJ 07753; in CANADA by H & L Pet Supplies Inc., 27 Kingston Crescent, Kitchener, Ontario N2B 2T6; Rolf C. Hagen Ltd., 3225 Sartelon Street, Montreal 382 Quebec; in ENGLAND by T.F.H. Publications Limited, 4 Kier Park, Ascot, Berkshire SL5 7DS; in AUSTRALIA AND THE SOUTH PACIFIC by T.F.H. (Australia) Pty. Ltd., Box 149, Brookvale 2100 N.S.W., Australia; in NEW ZEALAND by Ross Haines & Son, Ltd., 18 Monmouth Street, Grey Lynn, Auckland 2 New Zealand; in SINGAPORE AND MALAYSIA by MPH Distributors (S) Pte., Ltd., 601 Sims Drive, #03/07/21, Singapore 1438; in the PHILIPPINES by Bioi-Research, 5 Lippay Street, San Lorenzo Village, Makati Rizal; in SOUTH AFRICA by Multipet Pty. Ltd., 30 Turners Avenue, Durban 4001. Published by T.F.H. Publications, Inc. Manufactured in the United States of America by T.F.H. Publications, Inc.

1.
Origin

During the last few years fishkeeping as a hobby has become more and more popular. Technical knowledge of this subject has increased to such an extent that it is now possible to reproduce in the home almost any aquatic landscape complete with its life forms. Whether possessing a living coral reef in the sitting room or an ornamental pond in the garden, the aquarist can derive a great deal of pleasure from his hobby.

Ranchu or Maruko.

External Features

If one were to picture in the mind's eye the image of a typical fish, then the shape of the common Goldfish would not be unlike that image. It possesses all of the typical fish characteristics: streamlined body, scaly skin, gill plates, large lidless eyes, large mouth, and of course the necessary fins.

The fins of a fish have three main functions—stabilization, braking, and to a lesser extent, propulsion, the main propulsive power being provided by muscular contractions of the body and tail. The functions of the individual fins are as follows. *Dorsal and anal fins* act as stabilizers to prevent the body rolling. *Pectoral and ventral fins* are responsible for balancing, braking, turning, and some propulsion. The *caudal fin* provides for turning, stabilizing, and propulsion. It is the caudal fin that shows the greatest variation between varieties, appearing as single, paired, or any intermediate variation with ends pointed, rounded, squared or forked, short or long.

The absence of lungs and the presence of gills are the main features which separate the fishes from the higher vertebrates. Fishes obtain their necessary oxygen by drawing water in through the mouth and filtering it through delicate gill membranes. Oxygen is removed during this process and absorbed into the bloodstream, and the water, together with carbon dioxide and other wastes, is discharged at the rear of the gill plates. When the water is polluted or deficient

PARTS OF THE GOLD-FISH

1. Dorsal fin.
2. Lateral line.
3. Nasal appendage.
4. Gill cover (operculum).
5. Pectoral fin.
6. Anal fin.
7. Pelvic or ventral fins.
8. Caudal or tail fin.

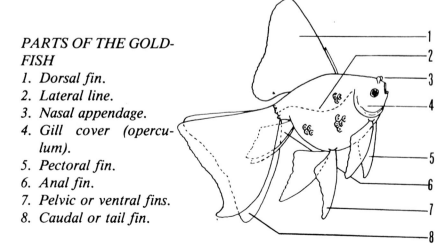

A mature Ranchu with the growth covering the entire head, gills, face . . . almost covering the eyes.

in oxygen, the fishes will congregate at the surface where oxygen is being dissolved into the water. When their gills make popping noises as they hang from the surface, they are gasping for air to avoid suffocation and require immediate attention.

Unlike the higher animals, the nostrils of fishes are simple pits containing scent buds and are in no way connected to either the respiratory or alimentary systems.

The Goldfish possesses no external ears but has instead a simple internal mechanism capable of picking up vibrations from the water.

The eyes of the fishes are large, lidless, and barely movable. The Goldfish does have adequate eyesight within a limited range but is generally believed to be nearsighted. The highly developed telescope and bubble eyes give an even more restricted field of vision.

The body of the Goldfish is covered with overlapping scales which are hard plates set beneath a thin layer of epidermal tissue for streamlining and protection against injury and infection. Mucous glands in the skin produce the characteristic slimy surface as a protective device—everyone knows how difficult it is to grasp a wriggling fish. The slimy surface also reduces skin friction that would retard movement.

The size of the scales varies with the size of the fish. Good shape and definition are important in creating the correct body outline. All Goldfish have scales but some are erroneously known as "scaleless." On these fish the scales are less conspicuous because they lack the layer of guanine which renders them opaque and gives them their metallic appearance. The amount of guanine apparent in a fish is governed partially by genetics and partially by the environment.

Fish that do not have this reflective substance under their scales are properly termed "matt", fish with guanine under all of their scales are termed "metallic", and fish with a combination of metallic and matt scales are termed "nacreous". Neither metallic nor matt scales are genetically dominant. Nacreous is the intermediate state of scale and is produced by breeding metallic to matt. Goldfish with matt scales, however, are seldom seen commercially because they do not show the intensity of color and the hardiness of the metallic fish. They are therefore often culled by commercial breeders.

Each variety of Goldfish will have a specific number of scales which will remain constant barring accidental loss. As the fish grows, so each scale grows at its periphery. Uneven growth caused by hibernation and restricted feeding produces ring formations on the scales which can be closely examined as indications of the age of the fish.

At 60 days of age most metallic fishes born with the protective Crucian coloring will usually begin to decolor. The scales will blacken and then the fish will begin to fade, starting at the ventral areas and progressing up to the dorsal fin. When a fish has completed this phase it will usually be yellow in color, but it may then darken considerably with the passage of time as the color intensifies. Not all Goldfish undergo this decoloring process; some may never discolor while others may not decolor until they are several years old. Matt fish never undergo this process because they are born light in color, often white, and they gradually darken as the colors intensify. The resulting color of a fish is affected by its diet and the environment as well as genetics.

2.
— Setting Up —

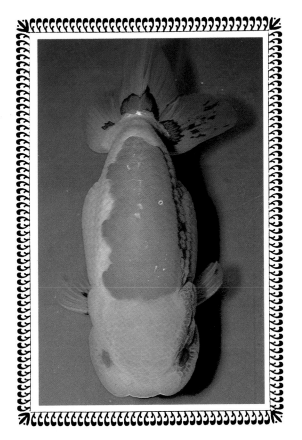

When purchasing a tank the first consideration should be exactly how many fish are to be housed. In order to maintain a good replacement of oxygen in the water the surface area must be as large as possible compared with the volume of the water. For example, two containers could hold the same volume of water but the surface area could vary considerably.

A magnificent Ranchu with pond markings that are best viewed from above.

To work out the capacity of a rectangular container in gallons, multiply the length of the tank by the height and then by the breadth. This will give the volume in cubic inches which can be converted to cubic feet by dividing by 1728 and then multiplying by 6¼. A formula for this could be expressed: $\dfrac{L \times H \times B \times 6¼}{1728}$.

Take for example a tank 36″ × 12″ × 12″. In this case the formula would become $\dfrac{36 \times 12 \times 12}{1728} = \dfrac{5184}{1728} =$ 3 cubic feet. The volume is therefore 3 cubic feet, which multiplied by 6-1/4 gives a capacity of 18-3/4 gallons.

(These calculations are based on the Imperial gallon, not the U.S. gallon.)

The figure which concerns us most, however, is the area of the water surface, which is found by multiplying the length by the breadth. We should allow 1″ of fish (not including the tail) for every 24 square inches of area. In the case of our 36″ x 12″ x 12″ tank, the surface area would be 432 square inches, which divided by 24 gives 18. This is therefore the number of inches of fish we can put in the tank. It does not matter how the inches are distributed as long as they add up to 18 (9 2-inch fish, 6 3-inch fish, or 2 4-inch and 2 5-inch fish). As the fish grow they must be thinned out to maintain the original 18 inches.

Before setting up a tank it is advisable to test it for leaks. Place the tank on a flat, solid surface and fill it with water. Leave it for several hours and then check for pools of water on the table top. If a leak occurs it may be repaired by using one of the many proprietary sealants available. Most modern glass tanks have already been sealed with one of these compounds and are therefore unlikely to leak.

FURNISHING THE TANK

The tank must now be furnished to make it attractive to look at and provide the fish with more natural conditions and some cover—even Goldfish feel more secure when they have a few places to hide.

Floor Covering

The first consideration is the floor covering, and aquarium gravel is most suitable for this. If too coarse a gravel is used uneaten food will lodge in the spaces between the stones and putrify the water.

Oranda, a lionhead with a dorsal fin, sometimes called a Goosehead or Turkeyhead. It originated in China.

If gravel is purchased from a pet dealer there will be no need to sterilize it, but it is still advisable to rinse out the dust.

When the gravel has been prepared it may be placed in the tank and sloped upward from the front of the tank to the back, approximately 2.5 cm (1 in.) at the front to 8 cm (3 in.) at the back. This slope will allow heavy debris to sink to the front of the tank where it can be easily seen and therefore removed before it causes any deterioration of the purity or clarity of the water.

Landscaping

Rocks may be placed in the tank to provide cover for the fish and render the whole setup more natural looking, and these should be sterilized by boiling. Care should be taken in the selection of rocks as many contain soluble substances toxic to the tank inhabitants. As a general rule avoid limestone and crystalline structures and use sandstone, flint, or granite. Suitable rocks are often offered for sale in pet shops. The rocks, which should not be too voluminous, are placed in position on the gravel. Where they are located and how they are arranged is best left to personal taste, but with the correct usage of materials it is possible to produce a natural looking landscape complete with miniature terraces and valleys.

Now is the best time to add water to the tank. Ordinary tap water is quite suitable as the small amount of chlorine it may contain will disperse within 24 hours. In order to avoid disturbing the gravel place a saucer on it and pour the water gently into the saucer. As soon as the tank is about one quarter full the rest of the water may be poured slowly without fear of disturbance.

The ultimate decoration in aquaria is living plants and there is no reason why the Goldfish aquarium should be without them. Plants not only beautify the display but also help to keep the water clear, provide extra oxygen, and absorb some of the carbon dioxide produced by the fish. It is not advisable to collect your own specimens from ponds and rivers as they may harbor parasites and disease germs.

Various types of plants are available from most tropical fish shops at a moderate price but there is room here to mention only a few of the many varieties. The following have been selected as particularly suitable for a Goldfish tank.

A Red-capped Veiltail.

Vallisneria is a grass-like plant, usually sold complete with roots for planting directly into the gravel. Most other plants are supplied as cuttings which will soon take root if given proper treatment. *Fontinalis* or Willow Moss is a pretty plant with tiny, dark green leaves. *Ceratophyllum* or Hornwort is a bushy plant with feathery leaves, ideal for cover. *Myriophyllum* or Milfoil is also an ideal aquarium plant but is quite often eaten by the fish unless they are uncrowded and well fed. *Elodea* is one of the fastest growers, ideal for a cold water aquarium. Before installing the plants they should be thoroughly washed under cold running tap water to remove any insects.

The best method of planting cuttings is to bind three or four sprigs together with lead (not copper) wire and then push them into the gravel using a forked stick. Be careful not to bind them too tightly or the wire will act as a tourniquet and prevent rooting. After two or three weeks the cutting should have rooted and this will be heralded by the appearance of new green shoots.

The planting skill required to construct a pleasant effect is acquired by trial and error and it may be necessary to move the plants several times before a satisfactory result is achieved. Usually the larger plants are placed at the rear and sides of the tank and the smaller plants more to the center. It is advisable to leave a plant-free swimming area towards the front of the tank so that the fish display themselves well.

Left: Giant Vallisneria; right, Corkscrew Vallisneria. Illustrations compliments of Tropica, Denmark.

From left to right: Elodea, Egeria densa; Lagarosiphon muscoides;
Hydrilla verticillata; Elodea canadensis.

It must be appreciated that all plants require sufficient light to photosynthesize and green water plants are no exception. The aquarium must therefore be placed in a fairly bright position, preferably near a window facing north or east, but on no account should a tank be placed in such a position that the midday sun can shine into it as this will overheat the water and kill both plants and fish.

During the winter months, extra artifical light must be provided as the reduced hours of daylight will be insufficient to keep the plants flourishing. This light may take the form of a low power bulb or strip light fixed into the aquarium lid. The handyman should be able to fix this up for himself, but if there is any doubt whatsoever call an electrician. The goal to aim for is a year 'round average of twelve hours of light per day.

When the tank is finally set up and planted, it is advisable to wait at least one week before introducing any fish. This will ensure that the plants have settled in and that the water has matured. Should the water become cloudy after a few days there is no cause for alarm as this is a completely natural phenomenon which will clear itself within a week, after which the fish may be introduced.

SELECTING A FISH

Unless you are dealing with a tropical fish store it is likely that the novice will be presented with a selection of the more common varieties of Goldfish from which to choose his stock. Fish are usually supplied as immature specimens that have not yet shown their inclinations towards the finer points sought after in mature fish and it will therefore be difficult to choose among them.

Regardless of the source, attention should be paid to the environment in which the fish are kept. The water should be clear, there should be no overcrowding in the tanks, and a pet dealer who allows dead fish to remain in the tanks should be shunned. The fish should be swimming freely and neither gasping for air at the surface nor clustered around the aerator. Examine the fish carefully for blemishes and torn fins and ensure that the fins are erect and the tails fanned out. The bottom of the fish should be gently rounded and concave. Slim specimens should be avoided.

Most fish today are transported in polyethylene bags and care should be taken that the fish is not exposed to extreme variations

Wakin, the common goldfish of Japan.

in temperature while in transit. Do not keep the fish inside the bag any longer than is necessary and, contrary to popular opinion, do not float the bag on the surface of the water to equalize the temperature. Pores in the polyethylene allow gas exchanges which can be positively harmful to the fish and it is therefore best to equalize the temperature by transferring the fish, together with the water, into a glass or metal container that will float on the surface of the tank or pond. If the quality of the water supplied with the fish is not suspect, then the fish may be allowed to swim free by lowering the edge of the container. If there is any doubt about the water, however, it is best to net the fish and gently lower the net into the aquarium, allowing the fish to swim free—never drop a fish onto the water surface.

When in doubt about the condition of a fish it is a good precaution to quarantine the fish for a week or so before introducing it into the established aquarium. The fish can be accommodated in an unfurnished tank where it can be closely observed for any indications of poor health.

Caution must be exercised when selecting fishes for a mixed aquarium as the larger fish may harrass and even eat the smaller ones, and the slow moving and delicate Celestials and Orandas will be out-maneuvred by the fast moving Comets at feeding time.

An Oranda with a full face mask growth.

3.
Aeration and Filtration

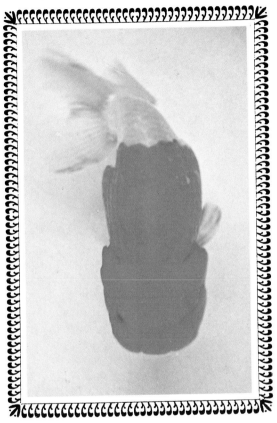

Now that the tank has been set up and planted and the fish have been introduced, regular maintenance should be a primary task. Obviously, when considerable time and patience has been devoted to making the aquarium as attractive and as natural as possible it is important that this be maintained. A well balanced tank should not require a great deal of upkeep, perhaps only thirty minutes per week, and it is best to set aside a certain time each week for this.

A Ranchu, a lionhead. Very colorful for top viewing.

Before continuing, however, a word of warning is necessary, as it is possible to "overmaintain" a tank—fish and plants will suffer if they are disturbed too often and this must be borne in mind.

After a few weeks, the aquarium will become "mature." This means that the correct rate of oxygen:carbon dioxide exchange has become established and it is at this time that algae will begin to appear in the tank. Algae is a low form of plant life, the spores of which can travel freely through both water and air and which will eventually find their way into any well-lit static water. There are many species of algae, some bright green in color and some reddish brown. All species of algae are advantageous in limited quantities as they provide some fresh food for the fish and help to oxygenate the water. The main problem with algae is that they grow on the inner glass surface of the aquarium and make it difficult to see the contents. It is therefore advisable to remove the algae from the viewing surfaces of the tank at weekly intervals. Special plastic scrapers may be purchased for this purpose, but it is also possible to make use of a razor blade. After scraping most of the algae off the inside of the glass, the surface should be wiped gently with a sponge until it is clear.

The next task is to examine the plants and remove any dead or dying leaves and shoots. These can be gently pinched off with the thumb and forefinger and removed from the tank. From time to time it may be necessary to prune those plants which have grown too large, and these cuttings may be retained for planting in another tank. Sometimes a mat-like algae (*Spirogyra*) will spread through the tank, covering rocks and plants with seemingly endless green threads. These should be removed by gently passing the fingers through the plant foliage, dragging out the weed and disposing of it.

During the week, a certain amount of sediment will build up on the surface of the gravel in the bottom of the aquarium, most of which will consist of dead pieces of plant, uneaten food, and fish droppings. Some of this will work its way into the gravel and provide nourishment for the plants, but the remainder, although relatively harmless to the fish, looks rather unpleasant and should therefore be removed. This is done by means of a siphon consisting of a short length of rubber hose. Put a bucket on the floor near the tank and immerse the siphon tube in the tank until it is filled with water. Now, leaving one end of the tube submerged in the tank,

A Ryukin, or Japanese Fantail.

block the other end with a finger, lift it out of the tank, and release it in the bucket. As long as the outlet end of the pipe is lower than the water level in the tank, the water will continue to siphon out. Hold the tube about half an inch from the surface of the gravel and move it around until all of the sediment has been siphoned out. Siphon off a quarter of the water from the tank. Restore the original water level by adding tap water that has stood at room temperature for four hours to ensure that the temperature difference is minimal.

Sometimes a layer of dust or scum will form on the water surface and this should be removed as it will prevent the efficient exchange of gases between the water and the atmosphere. Lay a single sheet of newspaper on the surface of the water and when it is thoroughly soaked gently remove it by slowly lifting it out of the water. Most of the scum will be lifted out with the paper.

After the aquarium has been flourishing for some time a few improvements may be desirable. Goldfish will live quite well in the conditions described so far but one may find that a little something is lacking; perhaps the water could be clearer or the fish healthier. At this point an aerator and a filter would be possible additions.

AERATION

The function of an aerator is to agitate the water and cause turbulence which exposes a greater surface area of water to the atmosphere while the air bubbles produced facilitate the absorption of oxygen. If certain river fish are kept in a tank, for instance the Golden Orfe, the Minnow, or the Stickleback, then an aerator would be a necessity as fish from fast flowing water demand more oxygen.

What then is an aerator? It is simply an apparatus that will introduce a regular supply of air into the tank of water. The two basic types of aerator are mechanical and nonmechanical.

Mechanical aerators are usually driven by electric motors and are either small air piston pumps or diaphragm vibrators. Both are available in various price ranges but the quieter and more efficient piston pump is usually more expensive. The piston pump has a longer working life and it will produce sufficient air for several aquariums. For the fancier with only two or three tanks, however, the diaphragm type should be quite adequate.

Whatever the method of aeration used, the air is conducted into the tank by a small gauge plastic tube to which an air stone has been attached. Air stones are manufactured from a porous material through which the air percolates and emerges as continuous streams of tiny air bubbles. The air stone can be hidden from view by placing it behind a rock. Sometimes airstones are lighter than water and will tend to float to the surface but this can be prevented by securing a pebble to the airstone with a rubber band.

FILTRATION

To keep the aquarium crystal-clear, a filter may be added. There are several types of filters available but the most practical is an air-lift filter that will utilize the existing aeration system. The principle of an airlift filter is that when air is released at the base of a tube immersed in water the air bubbles will push water up the tube and thus create a current. If this tube is placed in a container packed with a filter medium, then more water must be pulled through the medium to replace that which is being pushed up the tube. Simple plastic filters which fit inside the tank are available at very reasonable prices and they can be screened from view by rocks and plants.

Head-on view of an Oranda.

One of the most beautiful water gardens in Japan.
The larger pool contains Koi. These are large carp,
closely related to the goldfish. The other pools contain
goldfish. Rain water runoff is directed into the ponds
for frequent water changes.

4.
Pond Garden

Many varieties of Goldfish are at their best in outdoor ponds. The advantages of keeping fishes in ponds are considerable—there are no aeration problems as the large surface area allows a substantial interchange of gases to take place, plants will grow freely, and there will be plenty of beneficial natural foods available for the fish.

Top view of a Ranchu

Methods of Pond Construction

There are many methods of constructing a garden pond, but it is not a product that should be rushed into without first giving it serious thought. Three methods will be considered here, each having its own special merits, but the choice must be left with the individual.

Primary consideration must be given to the siting of the pond. It should not be constructed near trees as falling leaves in the autumn will cause endless trouble. Leaves must be continually removed or they will sink, decompose, and upset the balance of a mature pond. The ideal site for a pond is one that receives sunlight on about half of its surface for most of the day. This will ensure that the fishes always have access to shade and that the water does not become too hot.

Molded Ponds

The first type of pond to be described is a commercially produced or plastic pond. These are rigid forms molded into the shape of the intended pond. They are usually of an informal design, have varying depths, and are the simplest of ponds to set as all that is required is to excavate a hole roughly the same size as the mold. Care should be taken to exclude any sharp stones between the lining and the earth as the weight of water could damage the mold and cause leakage. When the mold has been set firmly into the ground and earth rammed into the empty space down the sides, the rim of the pond may be disguised with flat rocks. Rock plants may be planted around the edge to give it a more natural appearance.

Lined Ponds

The second type of pond is slightly more difficult to construct but it is also the cheapest. In fact, all one needs to purchase is a large sheet of thick gauge plastic. First dig out an area to the required shape and size. A minimum depth of 76 cm (2-1/2 feet) is recommended at the center of the pool, gently sloping to reach ground level at the edges. When the hole has been excavated the area should be raked carefully to smooth out the contours and remove stones. The plastic sheeting is then laid in the hole, with at least one foot of it bordering the edge of the pond. On this border are placed heavy rocks which will camouflage the sheeting and also hold it in place. The earth which has been excavated may be piled

Side and top views of the same fish. These Ranchu are prize-winning fish because of their uniform markings and the fact that the missing dorsal origin is almost invisible, as is the defective dorsal (back) profile. Further champion Ranchus are shown on page 31.

around the rear and possibly one or two sides of the pond to make a rockery. As the pond is filled, the weight of the water will press the sheeting into the contours of the hole, providing an excellent lining. Plants must be installed in pots or containers in this sort of pond so that their roots do not penetrate the plastic sheeting.

Concrete Ponds

The third and final type of pond to be described is the concrete pond. This is usually the most expensive and the most difficult to construct, but it is well worth it as it is definitely the most permanent and reliable. With careful planning and a few weekends' work, the enthusiast may construct a landscaped pond which will not only provide an ideal home for his fish but will also be an object of pleasure for many years.

First of all it must be decided whether the pond is to be formal or informal in design and this may well depend on the existing layout of the garden. A plan of the pond should then be drawn up and location, size, type of subsoil, and drainage considered before construction begins. A formal pond is usually slightly easier to construct because its sides are straight and simpler to cast. Mark out the shape of the pond on the site using pegs and string, remembering to take into account the thickness of the walls. Allow for the walls to slope slightly outward so that should the pond freeze over, the ice will push upward instead of forcing squarely against the walls of the pond.

A drain will be of considerable assistance when it comes time to empty the pond for cleaning. This should be situated at the deepest point in the pool and should allow the water to drain into either a main drain or a dry well. A bathtub plug will be adequate as a stopper and it is a good idea to have a piece of mesh positioned in the drain to prevent debris from clogging the pipe. The dry well should be three times the volume of the pool and should be filled with large stones and rubble, allowing the entire contents of the pool to be drained at once. It is quite satisfactory to have a small dry well and empty the bulk of the water first by siphon for general garden usage and when the pool is almost empty pull the plug and drain away the remainder.

An overflow is very useful in a downpour as it will retain a constant level in the pool and prevent it from flooding out and washing in

Champion Ranchus.

Closely related to goldfish are the Japanese Colored Carps called "Koi."

contaminating matter from the surrounding area. A vertical pipe connected to the drain can prove very satisfactory in maintaining the pond level. The pipe is screwed into a socket positioned in the drainage hole and then cut to the height of the desired water level. Any water above the top of the pipe will run into the drainage system, thereby maintaining a constant level in the pond. It is advisable to cover the end of the pipe with fine mesh to prevent any floating debris or unsuspecting fish from being pulled into the pipe.

The excavated earth should be piled well away from the edge of the pond. If the pond is to be formal in shape it is advisable to make three different levels, the shallowest being about 15 cm (6 in.) in depth and the deepest being approximately 76 cm (2-1/2 ft.). After the hole has been excavated you can either lay a lining of 100 gauge plastic sheeting or ram approximately three inches of rubble into the base.

The next step is the actual laying of the concrete and the cardinal rule to remember here is that the pool should be laid in a single operation, working from one end to the other, laying the base and sides as you go along. Do not lay the base one day and then lay the sides at a later date or you will find that the seams formed will be prone to leaks and encourage cracking should the pond freeze over. Shuttering for the sides of the pond should be made from wooden planks and these should be situated so that earth walls are the same distance from the shuttering all around the perimeter. An ideal concrete mixture is by volume one part cement, two parts sand, and three parts gravel or shingle. Using a hard, flat surface, mix the sand and cement together first and then mix in the gravel. Water should be added slowly until the desired consistency is reached, ensuring that it does not become too wet and runny to be easily manageable.

The thickness of the concrete will depend upon the size of the pond, but as a general rule make the base and sides of a 183 cm (6 ft.) wide by 122 cm (4 ft.) high by 76 cm (2-1/2 ft.) deep pond 10 cm (4 in.) thick and increase the thickness by 1 cm (1/2 in.) for every extra foot in length or width. Wire mesh may be set into the concrete while laying for reinforcement, taking care that it does not come through the surface. Concrete is rammed between the shuttering and the earth wall, ensuring that every cavity is filled. Allow 72 hours for the concrete to set before removing the shuttering. When the concrete has dried, paint the inside with cement. Do not allow this finishing coat to dry too quickly or it will not cure properly, and therefore cover the surface with damp burlap and shade it from direct sunlight. If there is the likelihood of rain soon after the laying of the concrete, it is a good idea to cover the pool with plastic. Once the cement has dried fill the pond with water and leave it for a week.

After the water in the pond has stood for about a week drain it completely, scrub the concrete surface with a stiff brush, rinse it out, and allow it to dry. To make the pond completely leak proof it is best at this stage to apply a coat of surface sealer. Several

Above: A lovely Ranchu with luxurious lionhead growth and an almost perfect profile on its back. The fish below is a nacreous Pearl Scale goldfish. The "pearls" will become more obvious as the fish gets older.

A Water Bubble-eyed goldfish, without a dorsal.

brands of sealer are manufactured especially for this purpose, all of which not only render the pond watertight, but also neutralize the effect of the lime in the cement which can be harmful to both fish and plants. The sealer should be applied following the manufacturer's instructions and allowed to dry. Fill the pool once more with water, leave it for a further 48 hours, drain, scrub, and rinse before preparation for stocking.

A path of irregular paving can be laid around the edge of the pond, and the excavated earth can be used for landscaping. With a little imagination the whole area can be made to blend in with its surroundings. It is simple to rig up a waterfall or fountain driven by a small electric pump and such an addition not only increases the attractiveness of the pond but is also an asset to the health of the fish.

Furnishing the Pond

In preparation for planting lay 5 cm (2 in.) of clean, coarse sand. The best time for planting is spring as this gives the plants a chance to establish themselves before winter sets in. There are many plants suitable for inclusion in a pond but most of them thrive at a depth of about 30 cm (1 ft.) and are best planted on shallow shelves provided for them. Plants may be purchased from your local pet shop where instructions on planting and care may also be obtained. No pond is really complete without a water lily or two and these are usually planted in submerged baskets near the center of the pond where they not only add a touch of beauty to the pond but also provide excellent hiding places for the fish.

After planting, the pond may be slowly filled with water. It is recommended that a heavy bucket be placed on the bottom of the pool and water slowly trickled into it to avoid disturbing the sand base. Before introducing the fish it is best to wait at least two weeks to allow the water to mature. When it has matured and the pond is ready for stocking introduce a few less valuable fish to test the water. A few fresh water snails in the pond are beneficial as they control the growth of algae to an extent and also act as scavengers. If the pond is to be used for breeding, however, snails are best left out as they will consume large quantities of fish eggs.

The maintenance of a well balanced pond is a simple matter. Fallen leaves must be removed from the surface before they sink to the bottom of the pond. It may be necessary to empty and clean a small pond every year. The best time to do this is late autumn after all the leaves have fallen. Plants should be thinned out, sludge removed, and the inside wall scrubbed down before refilling with water.

It is not necessary to change the sand and loam at the bottom of the pond unless the water has become polluted and the fish are dying. In this case the whole interior of the pond must be disinfected with household bleach and thoroughly washed out so that no trace of the bleach remains. Larger ponds need not be cleaned out every year but it is wise to do so at least every other year. Remember that when the water has been completely changed the fish should not be returned to it immediately as the water must mature. During cleaning periods the fish may be kept in well aerated tanks.

In the winter the surface of the pond may freeze over. The low temperatures will not harm the fish, but if the ice is left unbroken for long periods a serious lack of oxygen can result. Never break the ice by tapping it as this will cause shock waves in the water and possibly harm the fish. The best procedure is to make part of the pool ice-free by standing a hot kettle on it until the ice melts. If snow settles on the ice it should be swept off in order to admit maximum light.

It is not long after setting up a garden pond that various uninvited visitors appear. Many of these do no harm to the fish and in fact some, like mosquito larvae, bloodworms, and caddis fly larvae, are even beneficial as they are scavengers as well as valuable live food for the fish.

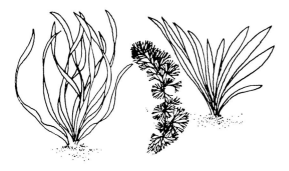

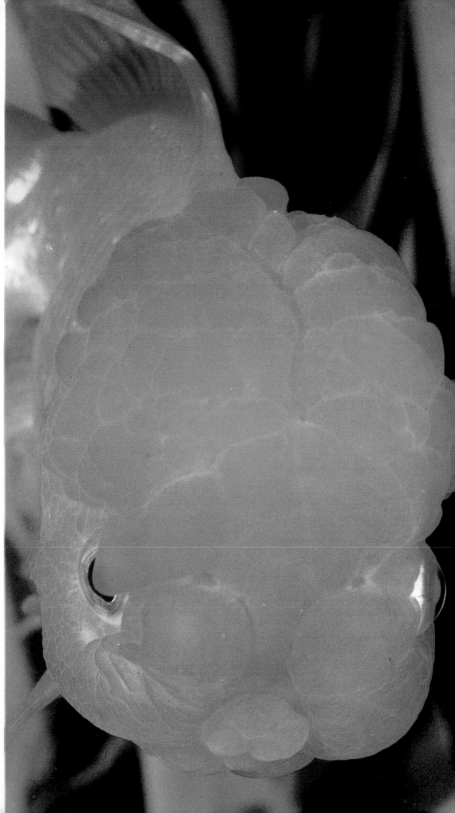

5.
Feeding

The foods fishes prefer vary tremendously among different species. Some are herbivorous, but the vast majority are omnivorous which means that they consume both animal and vegetable matter. The Goldfish and many other cold water species are omnivorous although they tend to consume more vegetable matter than animal. The basic diet of Goldfish should therefore be predominantly vegetable food supplemented with animal food.

Above: A fish whose eyes are always looking at heaven . . . a Celestial Goldfish. On the facing page is Aaron Norman's photo of an Oranda.

One of the most frequent causes of premature death among pet Goldfish is incorrect feeding. Overfeeding is one of the beginner's worst vices and it is something which the uninformed cannot seem to resist. Fish eat far less than one expects and if given more than they can immediately consume the food will sink to the bottom of the aquarium or pond and eventually pollute the water. Floating feeding rings are available that retain floating food in a restricted area so that uneaten food will fall within a small area that can be cleaned easily. As a general rule never give the fish more than they can consume in ten minutes. Also try to give them pieces of food which they can easily find and comfortably swallow, avoiding both small and excessively large particles.

Many excellent brands of dried foods which contain a complete balanced diet for fish are available on the market. They are sold in various forms—flakes, powders, and compressed tablets being the most common. All are designed especially for various types of fish and contain the correct proportions of carbohydrates, proteins, fats, vitamins, and minerals required to keep the fish in prime condition. It is as well to vary foods as much as possible in order to give the fish an assortment. "All purpose" foods may be supplemented with a little animal matter such as tubifex worms, shrimps, and ants' eggs. Goldfish have been known to live for years on a diet of dried food but they cannot compare in respect to growth, finnage, and color with fish whose diet has been supplemented with live food.

The value of live foods is never to be underestimated and it is well worth the extra trouble of obtaining various suitable invertebrates for this purpose. Some live foods such as tubifex, daphnia and brine shrimp are usually available in pet shops and the small quantities required may be obtained cheaply.

Earthworms are one of the most valuable live foods, especially during the breeding season, and they are almost always available. Whole earthworms are usually too big for any but the large pond Goldfish to consume and they must therefore be chopped into smaller pieces.

Microworms or "white worms" are another valuable food, especially for the smaller fish. Cultures of these can be purchased.

The correct feeding of fishes is very important and when possible they should be fed at the same times every day, preferably once in the morning and once in the evening. The food should always be placed in the same spot in the aquarium or pond and the fish will soon learn to anticipate feeding time. If for any reason a meal is missed this will cause no harm to the fish provided that this does not happen too often. Most fishes live quite happily for up to four weeks without being fed, and during this time they will obtain some nourishment by nibbling at the water plants and the algae, but such a course is not recommended.

As fishes are cold blooded creatures their rate of metabolism decreases at low temperatures and they require little food. In fact, if the temperature is below 10° (50°) they will not feed at all. Smaller quantities of food should be given during the cold spells and in the outdoor pond they need not be fed at all in the winter except during particularly mild spells. Foods containing high percentages of fats should be avoided in cold weather because they require considerable digestion and the metabolism of the fish will not be able to cope with them.

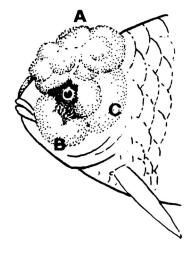

REGIONS ON A GOLD-FISH HEAD WHERE GROWTHS MAY OCCUR:
A. Cap
B. Cheek
C. Opercular region.

6.
Goldfish Types

Oranda

Similar in body shape to the Lionhead, the Oranda also has a warty growth covering its head, but on this fish the growth on the forehead is most pronounced. The hood becomes visible at approximately six to seven months of age.

Above: A very rare Calico Oranda; on the facing page is a Curly-tail Fantail . . . a very rare variety.

The Oranda has a very prominent dorsal fin and the caudal fin is similar to that of the Veiltail. Colors vary and include combinations of red, white, orange, yellow, gray, black, and blue.

Pompon

The Japanese Pompon has a body similar to that of an Oranda and has fleshy appendages or pompons hanging from its nostrils. The Chinese Pompon, or Narial Bouquet, has the body of a Lionhead and the growths from its nostrils are more rounded than those of the Japanese Pompon, moving noticeably as the fish swims.

Shubunkin

This handsome matt fish was first bred in Japan in 1900 and was soon introduced into Britain. It is single-tailed and somewhat resembles the common Goldfish in shape, but its coloration is exceptional. The background color is usually bright blue, this being unevenly blotched with intense black, red, gold, and brown. The translation of "Shubunkin" is "red brocade."

Two varieties of Shubunkin have been developed in the United Kingdom, the "London" and the "Bristol" both of which have similar coloration but different finnage. The fins of the London Shubunkin resemble those of the common Goldfish while the Bristol Shubunkin has a longer tail and a higher dorsal fin as seen in the Comet Goldfish. Both varieties of Shubunkin are hardy and will breed in large indoor tanks or in outdoor ponds.

Young Shubunkins assume adult coloration fairly rapidly and if well fed will reach sexual maturity in less than a year, but they are rather delicate up to the age of six months and should not winter in outdoor ponds under this age.

Comet Tail

The Comet Tail was developed in the United States at the end of the nineteenth century. It is red or red and white in color and the scales are metallic. The caudal fin is as long as or longer than the slender body and the dorsal fin is deeply concave and pointed at the rear. This hardy fish is one of the most active and will live and breed quite safely in an outdoor pond or aquarium.

Fantail

A plump, oval bodied fish, the Fantail is one of the more fancy varieties which will live in both the aquarium and the outdoor pond. It is one of the older varieties and is believed to have first appeared in Europe during the late sixteenth century. This fish is found in both metallic and matt versions, the latter often having the coloration of the Shubunkin. The main characteristic of the Fantail is the caudal fin which is about half the length of the body and has four lobes. The dorsal fin is high, the front part being almost vertical. The ventral fins are rather large and the anal fins are paired. The Fantail does not grow very large, averaging 8 cm (3 in.) in body length.

Veiltail

The Veiltail first appeared in the United States as a mutation of the Japanese Fantail. The paired caudal fins of the fish are approximately twice the length of the almost spherical body and should hang at an angle of 45° from the lateral line. The caudal fins should be squared off at the ends as if they had been cut by a knife, and indeed some competitors have been accused of doing just that. Veiltails have extremely high, sail-like dorsal fins about three quarters the height of the body, and their long paired anal fins should be partially hidden by the caudal fins. Both metallic and matt versions appear, the latter having the coloration of the Shubunkin.

The Veiltail is one of the less hardy Goldfish and should not be kept in an outdoor pond or in water at a temperature below 10°C (50°F). Veiltails require more protein than other varieties and should therefore be given a considerable amount of live food. They also require a large swimming area as in cramped conditions they tend to damage their delicate finnage.

Lionhead

This variety has a strange wart-like growth covering its head. Given the right conditions the growth becomes visible approximately four months after birth but the development of the growth depends to a great extent on the manner in which the fish are raised. Tubifex and bloodworms are fed in large quantities and the water is kept free from algae. To support a good "hood", fish with broad heads are preferred and considerable culling is necessary to obtain a few acceptable specimens.

Another peculiarity of the Lionhead is the lack of a dorsal fin—fish showing any trace of a dorsal fin are culled. The caudal fin is double and all other fins are short. Both metallic and matt Lionheads are available.

The Lionhead is very delicate and is often unnecessarily kept at temperatues in excess of 18°C (65°F). It is, however, recommended that the temperature be kept above 13°C (55°F) at all times. The hard warty growth makes the gill plates inflexible and places a strain on breathing and therefore well aerated water is essential.

Below is a Ranchu; on the facing page is a Red-capped Veiltail. These fish are called (mostly incorrectly) Gooseheads, Raspberry or Strawberry Heads, Turkeyheads, etc. This fish has had its photo appear in dozens of publications.

EXOTIC EYED GOLDFISH

The following varieties have highly developed eyes and require much individual attention. Care must be taken in feeding these fish as their limited vision often results in their finding food only when it is floating directly above them. Unless a great deal of time can be spent with these fish they are not recommended.

Telescope-Eyed Goldfish

Telescope-eyes are eyes elevated by fleshy protuberances and they are found on Fantail and Veiltail Goldfish. The characteristic appears when the fish are about one month of age and the eyes enlarge as the fish grow. The fish must be symmetrical and any imbalance in size or shape would make a fish inferior.

Black Moor

The Black Moor appears only with telescope eyes and in fact the black color seems to be linked genetically with telescope eyes. No all-black Goldfish have ever been found with normal eyes.

The Black Moor has the finnage of either the Fantail or the Veiltail and always has metallic scales. These fish are very delicate and cannot be kept in outdoor ponds. In aquariums they require a temperature of 16°C (60°F+) or more. Some Moors fade in color as they age and become bronzed.

Celestial

The main characteristic of the Celestial Goldfish is the protuberant eyes permanently fixed pointing skyward. They have no dorsal fin.

One Chinese fable tells that Celestials were developed in tribute to an Emperor—when he looked down into his pond to admire his fish he found them gazing adoringly up at him.

Bubble-eye

The Bubble-eye Goldfish has the body of a Lionhead Goldfish with bulges beneath each eye. It was initially bred to favor firm water sacs under the eyes but the trend is now towards loose bubbles that move as the fish swims.

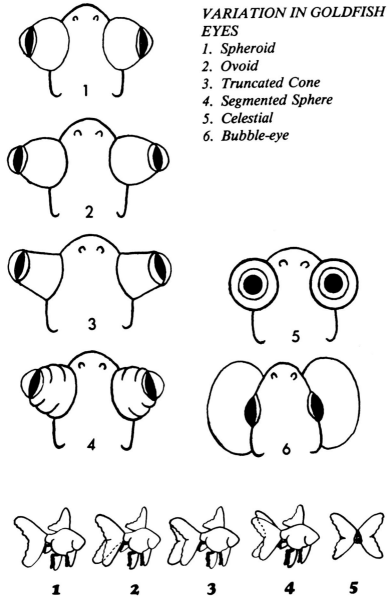

VARIATION IN GOLDFISH EYES
1. *Spheroid*
2. *Ovoid*
3. *Truncated Cone*
4. *Segmented Sphere*
5. *Celestial*
6. *Bubble-eye*

Variation in the Goldfish tail. English names are followed by Japanese translation.

1. Singletail/*Funa-wo*
2. Tripod tail/*Tsumami-wo*
3. Webtail/*Mitsu-wo*
4. Double tail/*Yotsu-wo*
5. Butterfly tail/*Kujaku-wo*

Above: A pair of Red Telescope-eyed goldfish spawning. Below: A pair of Japanese Pompon Orandas with both the nasal appendages hanging from its nostrils and the Oranda body and head. The fish are spawning.

7.
Breeding

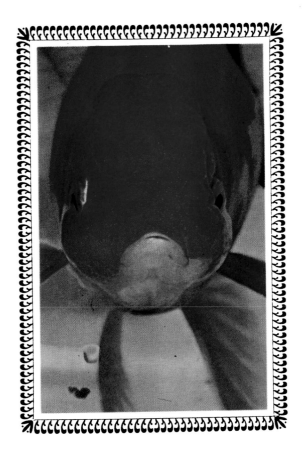

Goldfish which have been kept in well aerated containers and fed correctly will reach sexual maturity at one year of age but they are not worth considering as breeders until they are two years old. After four years of age their abilities as good breeders decrease with large, deformed, and infertile eggs being common.

A head-on view of an Oranda.

In the autumn the breeders should be given a predominantly vegetable diet but in the spring the adult fish should be given a large proportion of live food. This not only stimulates the sex drive but also helps to ensure a good breeding result. Fish will not spawn in crowded conditions and it is therefore important that they be given ample room.

It is rather difficult to sex Goldfish outside the breeding season from May to August, but during this period the females become plump with eggs and the males develop small whitish tubercles on their gill plates and pectoral fins. Even if these small bumps cannot be easily seen they can usually be felt with a gentle finger. Females tend to be slightly larger than males of the same age.

As spawning time approaches it is wise to separate the males from the females in order to prevent spawning activity before you are prepared for it. Ensure that there are no plants in with the females or some may release their eggs even though there is no hope of their being fertilized. This separation also intensifies their interest in one another when they are finally reunited.

If many varieties of fish are kept in the same pond, interbreeding will occur. This is often termed "random breeding" and is not recommended as eventually over a period of years all of the fish will revert back to the appearance of the wild Goldfish. All Goldfish have common ancestors and it is therefore possible for all of the different varieties to breed with each other. Even with careful selective breeding of a given variety many inferior fish will be produced, but it would be a shame to allow the centuries of hard work by dedicated breeders who have tried to produce varieties to breed "true" to be undone in a few generations.

Selective breeding is the method preferred by most aquarists. This means that Goldfish of only one variety are allowed to mate with each other and therefore the young fish will be similar to their parents. To produce really good offspring the best parent fish are selected—those showing the desirable characteristics of their variety.

Nests

Eggs are naturally deposited on the plants in the shallow waters at the edge of the pond and it is therefore essential to ensure that suitable nesting material is available. Nests can consist of bunches of water plants, dried willow roots, or nylon mops. The main advantage of non-living nesting material is that it can be sterilized to ensure that no pests are introduced into the pond. The fish will be stimulated into spawning by rubbing themselves against the nesting material and it should therefore not be added until you are prepared to care for the eggs. The nesting material should not be located deeper than 30 cm (12 in.) or many of the fry will not survive. Eggs require considerable oxygen and it is therefore important that they do not sink into the mud. Ensure that there is no decaying material in the pond that would deplete the oxygen supply.

POND BREEDING

In outdoor ponds the male fish will select their own mates and much chasing will occur, usually in the shallow parts of the pond. You will find that some of your males will be rather unenthusiastic in this respect, usually a higher percentage in the more exotic varieties, and it is a good precaution to provide more males than females. A ratio of three males to each female would assure a high fertility rate in the eggs.

The object of the chasing activity appears to be a desire on the part of the male to bump the underside of the female with his nose in a endeavor to help her to release the eggs. To counteract this and no doubt to excite the male further, the female sinks to the bottom of the tank. As she is forced to rise, the male continues to lift her until she is on top of the plants and almost out of the water. As spawning approaches, this courtship becomes more violent and is a good advance warning that spawning will shortly follow. In the more exotic varieties, however, this phase is sometimes omitted and spawning can come as a complete surprise to the breeder.

One evening when the chasing is in full swing place the nests in the water. Spawning usually occurs the following morning soon after the morning light reaches the pond. If possible put the nests into the water when it is likely that the weather will remain warm for a few days.

When the female accepts the male she will start laying eggs among the water plants or nesting material. These are laid singly, each one being about the size of a pin head. The sticky surface of the egg enables it to fasten onto the leaves of the water plants and during this time the male will follow the female, spraying each egg with milt to fertilize it.

The above assumes that all is well, but sometimes the fish do not spawn because they are not ready for breeding, the water temperatue drops, or the fish have not accepted their new surroundings if they have recently been moved to a special breeding pond.

Hatching

If only a few fry are required, then the eggs can be left in the pond with the parent fish. Many eggs and hatchlings will be consumed by the adults, but in a well planted pond some will always escape and reach maturity.

Japanese have been intrigued for centuries by the exotic beauty of goldfishes. This is a 300-year-old print of a pair of Telescope-eyed Fantails spawning.

Those who wish to raise greater numbers of fry should remove the nests for hatching in special tanks. A fish will spawn several times in a season, each time releasing approximately 2,000 eggs, so unless you are concentrating on obtaining sheer numbers of fish it is best to collect only the first eggs laid, the ones which are considered by many breeders to be superior.

Hatching tanks can be of almost any material and size from glass aquarium tanks to plastic bread bins. The depth of water should be about 30 cm (1 ft.) and there are no special floor covering requirements. The tanks should receive some natural sunlight, and it is best to maintain the water temperature between 18°C (65°F) and 21°C (70°F). This can be accomplished by using special thermostatically controlled aquarium heaters. Do not attempt to put eggs that have been spawned on different days in the same hatching tank because the difference in size of fry will be considerable and the large fish will be quite happy to dine on the smaller ones.

A day or two after spawning some of the eggs will be seen to have turned white and these will be the eggs that are infertile. The infertile eggs can encourage the growth of fungus and it is therefore a good idea to remove them if you are working on a small scale.

Depending upon the water temperature, the fertile eggs should hatch in four to fourteen days—the warmer the water the quicker the hatching. Four to five days is ideal and any considerable extension of this is undesirable.

Care of Fry

Newly hatched fry are very delicate and should not be netted or moved. They could be killed by even a small drop in temperature and dust on the water surface could prevent them from breaking the surface.

There is no need to feed the fry during the first two days after hatching as they will live off their egg yolks, but as soon as these have been absorbed they will become free swimming and feed ravenously. For the first four weeks, Goldfish fry can feed only upon the most minute particles. In an open pond, the fry will find their own food, algae and small organisms being in plentiful supply, but if the fry are to be raised in tanks then it will be necessary to feed them small quantities of food several times a day.

Many foods are suitable for Goldfish fry, the most common being suspended algae in the water. To obtain an algae suspension an old glass aquarium tank is filled with water and left outdoors. After about a week the water will become green with suspended algae. To feed this to the fry remove a pint of water from the fry tank and replace it with a similar quantity of the suspension. While the fry are still transparent there is a risk of their swallowing algae which in strong sunlight will continue to grow and expand within the stomach. To minimize the risk of this, shade the water during periods of extreme sunlight.

Cultures of Infusoria which can be produced in jam jars are also excellent food for fry. Jars are filled with water to which a pinch of garden soil and a bruised lettuce leaf or a few strands of straw have been added. After a few days in a warm place the Infusoria, which are a collection of semi-microscopic organisms, will be seen as a moving cloud in the jars. A few drops of the culture added to the rearing tanks several times a day will provide nutritious food for the fry.

Finely sieved daphnia are by far the best food for young fry and newly hatched brine shrimp are also excellent.

A suspension of hard boiled egg yolk in water is also a valuable standby but should be given sparingly so that the water does not become polluted. Almost all of the adult Goldfish foods may be given but they must first be ground to a fine powder or made into a paste.

As the young fish reach four weeks of age they should begin to take larger food particles. If they have been fed properly they will, at this stage, be about 2.5 cm (1 in.) in length and capable of taking daphnia, tubifex, and whiteworm, as well as adult Goldfish food. At this stage they should be thinned out, all runts and deformed specimens being discarded. Ensure that the tanks do not become overcrowded by moving surplus fish to other tanks.

When they are about six months of age the young fish should be about 5 cm (2 in.) in length and start to assume the adult coloration. Those fish which have been raised in indoor rearing tanks should not be placed in an outdoor pond until the following spring.

AQUARIUM BREEDING

So far, the rearing of pond produced eggs and fry has been described, but for controlled selective breeding it is necessary to pair the fishes in aquarium tanks. The best method is to prepare the tank with a glass partition across the center. Clean gravel is placed on the floor and one end is provided with a loose tangle of water plants, Elodea being ideal for this purpose.

The tank is then filled with water and allowed to stand for twenty-four hours before the introduction of the selected pair of fish. The female is placed in the side containing the plants and the male is placed in the clear compartment. If the fish are in breeding condition they will begin to take obvious interest in each other after a few days. When the attention is noticed the glass partition is removed and the water level lowered to about six inches in depth. The best time to do this is late evening and it will usually be found the following morning that the fish have already spawned. If they have not spawned, they should be left together for a few days but if they then fail to spawn, it is advisable to repeat the divided tank procedure. If after repeated attempts the fish still refuse to spawn it is obvious that the fish are incompatible and must therefore be replaced with another pair. With the novice breeder it is worth considering that you may have tried to mate two fish of the same sex.

When the fish have spawned they must be removed from the tank as soon as possible before they have a chance to eat the eggs. This is a much greater hazard in a confined aquarium than a large pond. The eggs may be either left in the breeding tank to hatch or removed to a hatching tank, but in either case a temperature of 21°C (70°F) and good aeration should be maintained.

A Black Moor goldfish.

8.
Health Care

Goldfish are by nature very hardy and adaptable creatures and when they succumb to parasites, fungi, or virus infections it is usually because they have been weakened by a poor environment—always the fault of the keeper.

A Red Koi carp.

Symptoms to watch for in your Goldfish are:

1. Loss of appetite
2. Sluggish and aimless swimming
3. Folded dorsal or caudal fin
4. Hanging from the surface or lying on the bottom
5. Slow reactions to disturbances
6. Rubbing against surfaces as if trying to scrape something off its body
7. Loss of luster
8. Ragged fins, lesions, spots, or bumps
9. Bloating or emaciation
10. Gills that are pale rather than flushed a healthy red

Should you notice your fish exhibiting any of the above symptoms consider carefully what might have caused trouble:

1. Have you introduced any new fish or plants into the aquarium or allowed water of doubtful purity to be added, possibly introducing parasites or diseases?
2. Is there adequate aeration? Are your fish overcrowded, or has their environment deteriorated generally?
3. Have you handled your fish roughly or changed the water without proper caution?
4. Have you been feeding inferior or improper foods or polluting the water by adding more food than the fish can eat?
5. Have the fish been receiving insufficient sunlight or have they been left to "cook" in a window?

Consider the above points carefully as they might give you a clue as to what is wrong with the fish. Often troubles can be cured simply by remedying the flaw in the environment, but sometimes chemical treatment is necessary.

Medicines can be administered either by direct application to the affected area or by dissolving the medicine in the water. If the substance is to be dissolved ensure that there are no particles remaining or these may be eaten by the fish with disastrous results. If you are in any doubt in this respect the solutions can be filtered before adding them to the tank.

Many proprietary drugs are available for specific problems and the average aquarist is usually well advised to stick to these, but be wary of any substance that is claimed to be a cure for everything.

If individual fish are suffering, isolate them immediately, but if the entire pond or aquarium is affected then large scale measures must be taken. If the exact trouble is not known then general first aid measures must be taken. Maintain a water temperature of 15.5°C (60°F), ensure adequate aeration, and feed only live food. Lower the water level to 8-10 cm (3-4 in.) so that distressed fish do not have to struggle to reach food and the well-oxygenated surface water.

Hospital Tank

If individuals require treatment they must be isolated from the rest of your stock to prevent possible spread of the malady with a resulting epidemic. A small hospital tank for this purpose should be unfurnished, have a stable temperature, and be situated in a quiet place away from bright lights where the fish will not be excited or disturbed. When you transfer the fish to this tank include as much of its original water as possible to minimize the shock.

An isolation tank prevents a sick fish from infecting healthy fish, the aquarium plants will not be damaged by chemicals, and more accurate doses can be administered because of the small volume of water. Healthy fish will not be able to harass weakened individuals, and once treatment is completed the tank can be easily sterilized.

Aquariums and Ponds

A fish that was feeling under the weather in an aquarium would soon be noticed, but in a pond where there are many fish and many places for them to hide it is not so easy to detect the symptoms until quite a few fish have been affected. The pond keeper must be extra vigilant, and if any fish comes to attention as being slightly off color it should be dipped out and placed in a container for individual attention.

Some problems are more likely to affect ponds than aquariums but are much more likely to be noticed in aquariums. Treatments for ponds and aquariums are basically the same, but of course the dosage must be increased for ponds in proportion to the volume of water.